Keep Yourself Safe

Being Safe
Out and About

Honor Head

W
FRANKLIN WATTS
LONDON•SYDNEY

Franklin Watts
Published in paperback in Great Britain in 2018 by The Watts
Publishing Group

Picture Credits: Cover, 1 © Shutterstock; 4, 5, 6, 7, 8, 9, 10, 11, 12, 13, 14,
15, 16 top, 17, 18, 19, 20 bottom © Dollar Photo Club; 16 bottom © ??/
iStock 19 top © Michael Luhrenberg/iStock

Series Editor: Eloise Macgregor
Series Designer: Alix Wood
Illustrations: Alix Wood

Every attempt has been made to clear copyright. Should there be any
inadvertent omission please apply to the publisher for rectification.

Dewey number 613.6
ISBN 978 1 4451 4438 2

Printed in China

Franklin Watts
An imprint of
Hachette Children's Group
Part of The Watts Publishing Group
Carmelite House
50 Victoria Embankment
London EC4Y 0DZ

An Hachette UK Company
www.hachette.co.uk

www.franklinwatts.co.uk

Contents

Hi!
I'm Safety Sam.
I'll help you learn
how to stay safe
out and about.

SS

Great outdoors

There's no excuse not to get out. If it's cold, wrap up warm. If it's hot, remember to put on suntan lotion – then get out and have fun!

Getting out and about is good for you whether it's walking the dog, playing football in the park, or having a picnic. It's good to keep fit and get some fresh air.

Stick to places where there are other people, such as your local park. Arrange to be with friends and family when you go out and about.

Ask Safety Sam

What should I take with me when I go out?

- Make sure you know your address and home phone number, or the mobile number of an adult you can call if something goes wrong.

- Make sure you have the address and telephone number of where you're going.

- Have enough money for a taxi or a phone call for emergencies.

- If you have a mobile, take it with you.

BEWARE

Don't only keep important numbers on your mobile. You may lose your phone. Keep them on a piece of paper with you, or try to remember them.

Safe route

Plan your journey especially if you are going somewhere new. If you are taking public transport look up the times of trains or buses there and back before you set off.

There is usually a timetable at the bus stop. You can also pick up a printed timetable at your local train or bus station. Or check an online timetable.

Avoid short cuts through narrow alleys, empty parks and empty underpasses or tunnels. If a stranger offers to give you a lift, say a firm 'no' and walk on.

Ask Safety Sam

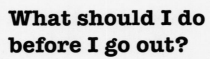

What should I do before I go out?

- Tell an adult where you're going and the route you are going to take.

- Tell them what time to expect you back.

- Make sure your mobile is charged. Put **safe numbers** on speed dial.

Road sense

Crossing roads can be very dangerous. When you are out, always choose a safe place to cross the road.

Safe places to cross the road are traffic lights, **zebra** and **pelican crossings** or where there is a **lollipop person** to stop cars for you.

Ask Safety Sam

If there is no pedestrian crossing, where can I cross?

- Cross where you can see the road clearly both ways. Look both ways to make sure the road is clear before you cross.

- Avoid corners or walking out from behind parked cars where drivers might not see you.

- Watch out for cyclists and motorbikes.

BEWARE

If you are walking on busy streets and crossing roads you need to know what's going on around you. This means not wearing headphones or talking on your mobile.

Play safe

Visiting the local playground, kicking around a football or skateboarding are all great exercise so get together with friends and get out!

Look for skate parks, parks and play areas with lots of other children and adults.

At the playground and skate park, wait your turn to have a go and don't push or get in the way of others.

At the playground, be careful not to walk too close to people on the swings or you could get hit by accident. If an adult you don't know asks to join in your game, be polite but say 'no'. If the stranger won't leave you alone, tell an adult you know.

Ask Safety Sam

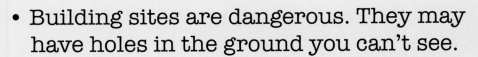

Where is it dangerous to play?

- Building sites are dangerous. They may have holes in the ground you can't see.

- Never, ever climb on scaffolding. You could easily slip and fall.

- Don't go in empty old buildings. They may have rotten floors that could collapse, or you may get trapped inside by accident.

- Never play near electricity **pylons**.

Water – beware!

If you are going out near a pond, lake, river or canal, be careful not to get too close. The water's edge can be muddy and you could easily slip. Even if you can swim, you are in danger of drowning.

If you want to play with boats or go fishing, make sure you have an adult with you. Never try and rescue anything that has gone into the water, such as a ball. If a person falls in the water, get help. Never try and rescue them yourself.

Ask Safety Sam

Why are ponds, lakes and streams dangerous?

- Drinking water from a stream, pond or lake can make you very sick even if the water looks clean.

- Some ponds and streams can be much deeper than they look.

- Some water can look very **calm**, but it can still be dangerous.

BEWARE

During the winter, the water in some ponds and lakes might freeze and become ice. Do not step onto the ice. It could easily crack and then you could fall under the ice.

Swim safe

Swimming is great exercise. Follow a few rules to stay safe and have fun. If you are at the beach or outdoor pool, don't forget the suntan lotion!

At the swimming pool don't run around the edge as you could easily slip. It is dangerous to jump or push other people into the pool. If you are out paddling or boating, always wear a **lifejacket** even if there are lots of other people about.

BEWARE

On the beach, swim where there is a **lifeguard**. Keep a look out for red flags which mean it is dangerous to swim in that spot.

Ask Safety Sam

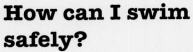

How can I swim safely?

- Only swim in a pond, lake, canal or river if it has a special swimming area and there are plenty of adults around.

- Don't jump in a river or the sea from rocks. You don't know what's under the water or how deep it is.

- At the swimming pool, stay at the shallow end if you are not a good swimmer.

Train safe

Never walk along a railway track, use one as a shortcut or play 'chicken' on a train track.

Level crossings are the barrier that come down and blocks your way onto the track when a train is due.

If the barriers are down, do not cross the track even if you can't see or hear a train. Modern trains are fast and quiet and you may not hear one coming. Never, ever play on a railway track.

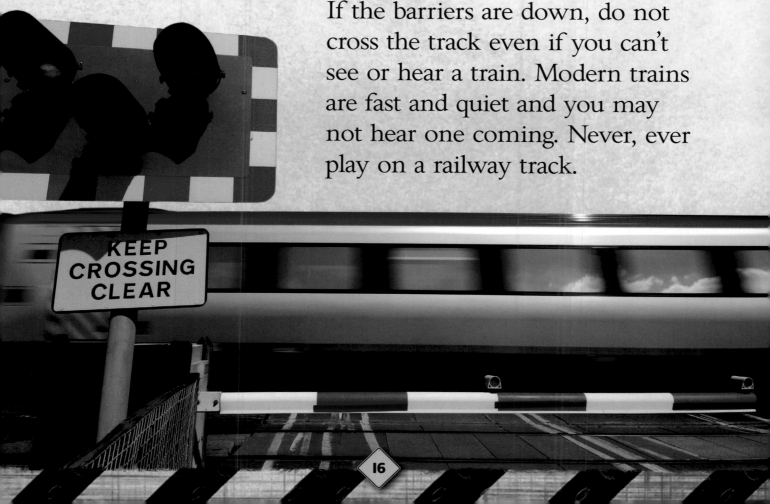

KEEP CROSSING CLEAR

Ask Safety Sam

How do I cross train tracks safely?

- Cross at a level crossing barrier if there is one.

- Don't go under the barrier to get across in a hurry – wait until the barrier has gone up.

- Some tracks have a bridge or an **underpass** you can use to cross the track.

BEWARE

When you are waiting for a train at the underground or train station, stand well back from the edge of the platform. Stand back while the train doors are being opened.

After dark

It can be much harder to spot dangers such as speeding cars once it's dark. Only cross the road at a pedestrian crossing or where there is lots of street light.

Ask Safety Sam

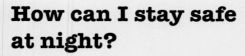

How can I stay safe at night?

- Keep a small torch in your bag and make sure the battery is working.

- Travel with friends. On a bus sit downstairs near the driver.

- Don't take shortcuts through a park or an empty open space that doesn't have any lighting.

Make sure you take a route that is well-lit with shops and people about. Walk in the middle of the pavement.

BEWARE

If you are going to be out after dark, wear bright or **reflective** clothing, especially if you are riding a bike.

Keep safe quiz

Answer the questions to check if you remember how to stay safe out and about.

1. What should you do if you are going somewhere new?
   a. Plan your route
   b. Go with friends
   c. Make sure you have water with you

2. What should you do to stay safe near water?
   a. Wear wellington boots
   b. Don't go near the water's edge
   c. Wear reflective clothing

3. Where is the best place to cross a rail track?
   a. Near the station
   b. A level crossing
   c. Where there are lots of people

4. If you are out in the dark, what should you wear?
   - a. Comfortable shoes
   - b. A hat
   - c. Bright or reflective clothing

Safety Sam Says

When you go out to play with your friends, where are the safest places to go? What are the dangerous places to avoid?

Glossary

calm When water is calm it looks flat and smooth and is not moving.

lifeguard A person who keeps watch at the swimming pool or on the beach to make sure people stay safe.

life jacket A special jacket that keeps you afloat if you fall in the water.

lollipop person A person who helps children to cross the road safely.

pelican crossing A crossing place with lights that turn red so the traffic stops.

public transport Buses, trams and trains.

pylons A tall tower-like structure carrying electricity cables high above the ground.

reflective Light bounces off reflective material, so that it shines and people can see you in the dark.

suntan lotion Cream that protects your skin from the sun.

safe numbers Phone numbers of people you should call in an emergency.

timetable A list showing when buses, trains and trams leave and arrive at all their stops.

underpass A passageway for people to walk under a busy road or railway line.

zebra crossing Black-and-white stripes marked on the road where cars usually stop to let people cross.

Answers from page 20-21
1) a 2) b 3) b 4) c

Further Information

Books

Giles, Sophie, *The Children's Book of Keeping Safe* (Little Learners), Award Publications, 2012.

Oxlade, Chris, *Be a Survivor*, Hungry Tomato, 2015.

Websites

Information on loads of topics including stranger danger
kidshealth.org/

Quizzes and tips on how to stay safe out and about
www.juniorcitizen.org.uk/kids/

Every effort has been made by the publisher to ensure that these websites contain no inappropriate or offensive material. However, because of the nature of the Internet, it is impossible to guarantee that the content of these sites will not be altered. We strongly advise that Internet access is supervised by a responsible adult.

Index